Published By Adam Gilbin

@ Tyler Hahn

Time Management: Your Time and Get Everything

Done a Practical Guide to Time Management and

Planning

All Right RESERVED

ISBN 978-87-94477-62-8

TABLE OF CONTENTS

Chapter 1 1

Understanding The Value Of Time 1

The Concept Of Time: A Finite Resource.......................... 1

Chapter 2 5

Performance Metrics And Continuous Improvement In Inventory Management 5

Chapter 3 20

Understanding Stress In The Modern World 20

Chapter 4 27

Goals.. 27

Chapter 5 37

The Importance Of Time Management In A Busy Professional's Life.. 37

Chapter 6 40

Basics Of Time 40

Chapter 7 47

The Benefits Of Good Time Management Include:........ 47

Chapter 8 56

Techniques For Evaluating Task Importance And Urgency
.... 56

Chapter 9 64

Breaking Down Long-Term Goals Into Manageable Tasks
.... 64

Chapter 10 77

Understanding Time Management: 77

Chapter 11 83

Understanding Time Management Fundamentals 83

Chapter 12 94

Recognizing Time Management 94

Chapter 1

Understanding the Value of Time

The Concept of Time: A Finite Resource

Money and possessions are not like time. Time is like a currency that goes away once spent. Time is fleeting, which makes every moment precious. For us to appreciate the value of time, we need to understand the finite nature of time. If we understand how limited time is, we can make conscious choices about investing our time.

Activity: Reflecting on Time

Take a moment to contemplate the concept of time. Consider its fleeting nature and the impact it has on your daily life. Document your thoughts in a journal to note how your ideas of time affect your decisions and actions.

The Importance of Managing Time for Personal and Professional Success

Effective time management is the foundation for building personal and professional success. It equips one to achieve their goals, complete their duties, and pursue their passions. In business, time management can be the gap between a thriving business and a struggling one. Time management aids productivity, ensures timely delivery, and aids a positive work ethic.

Successful Time Management in Business

Explore real examples of people who have achieved success through time management practices. Analyze their strategies and draw inspiration from their efficient journeys.

Typical Time Wasters and Pitfalls

In mastering time, try to identify time-wasting habits and pitfalls that hinder productivity. These include Procrastination, lack of prioritization, excessive multitasking, and failure to set boundaries. There are more examples of challenges one faces, discover yours and work on it. I used to surf the internet for more hours than I should and then wonder where all the time has gone.

Identify these obstacles, tackle them, and pave the way for effective time management.

Exercise: Identifying Your Time Wasters

Create a list of activities or habits that often waste your time. Be honest with yourself. Once identified, create a strategy to cut or drop these time wasters from your routine.

Summary

Understanding the value of time is the foundational step toward mastering its management. In this chapter, we talked about the nature of time and its gain on our personal and professional success. Also, we discussed common pitfalls that can hinder effective time management. You are now equipped to embark on the transformative journey of maximizing your time.

In the next chapter, we will look at the steps for Setting Clear Goals. This is a crucial element in effective time management. By defining your goals with care, you create a roadmap that guides your actions and decisions. This ensures that your time is purposeful and meaningful.

Chapter 2

Performance Metrics and Continuous Improvement in Inventory Management

In the ever-evolving world of inventory management, it is crucial to establish and monitor performance metrics to drive continuous improvement. These metrics serve as objective measures to evaluate the effectiveness and efficiency of your inventory management practices. By tracking and analyzing these key performance indicators (KPIs), you can identify areas for improvement, make informed decisions, and optimize your inventory processes.

Inventory Turnover:

Inventory turnover is a fundamental metric that measures how quickly your inventory is being sold and replaced over a specific period of time. It indicates how efficiently you are managing your inventory levels and how well you are meeting customer demand. A higher inventory turnover ratio typically suggests effective inventory management and minimizes the risk of obsolete or deadstock.

To calculate inventory turnover, divide the cost of goods sold (COGS) by the average inventory value during a given period. A higher turnover indicates that your inventory is being sold quickly, which helps generate cash flow and reduce carrying costs. However, it is essential to strike a balance, as excessive turnover might indicate a lack of inventory availability or missed sales opportunities.

Gross Margin Return on Investment:

GMROI is a metric that links inventory performance to profitability. It measures the return on investment (ROI) generated from the sale of inventory, taking into account both sales revenue and the cost of goods sold (COGS). By calculating GMROI, you can assess the profitability of your inventory investments and identify areas where adjustments may be required.

To calculate GMROI, divide the gross margin (sales revenue minus COGS) by the average inventory value during a given period, and then multiply it by 100. A higher GMROI indicates that your inventory investment is generating strong profitability. It helps measure the balance between sales revenue, inventory costs, and profit margins. Monitoring GMROI regularly enables you to evaluate the effectiveness of your inventory decisions and identify opportunities to optimize your product mix, pricing, and procurement strategies.

Fill Rate:

Fill rate measures the percentage of customer orders that are completely filled from available inventory. It reflects your ability to meet customer demand promptly and accurately. A high ll rate indicates strong customer service and e cient inventory control, while a low ll rate may lead to dissatis ed customers and lost sales.

To calculate ll rate, divide the total number of complete orders by the total number of orders received, and then multiply it by 100. An ideal ll rate is generally considered to be above 95%. Monitoring ll rate allows you to identify potential issues in your order processing, inventory availability, or forecasting accuracy. By maintaining a high ll rate, you improve customer satisfaction, reduce order cancellations or returns, and enhance your reputation as a reliable supplier.

Order Accuracy:

Order accuracy measures the percentage of orders that are processed correctly without errors or discrepancies. It ensures that the right items are shipped in the right quantities and to the right locations. Improving order accuracy reduces costly returns, customer complaints, and related operational ine ciencies.

To calculate order accuracy, divide the number of correctly processed orders by the total number of orders, and then multiply it by 100. Aim for an order accuracy rate close to 100%. Regularly monitoring order accuracy allows you to identify and address issues such as picking errors, misplacements, or system integration problems. Enhancing order accuracy not only improves customer satisfaction but also reduces unnecessary costs associated with incorrect shipments and reshipments.

Stockout Rate:

The stockout rate measures the frequency of inventory stockouts or situations in which desired products are unavailable when customers request them. A high stockout rate indicates inadequate inventory forecasting, replenishment, or management, which can lead to lost sales, dissatis ed customers, and reduced pro tability.

To calculate the stockout rate, divide the number of stockouts by the total number of customer orders, and then multiply it by 100. A stockout rate below 5% is generally desirable. By monitoring the stockout rate, you can identify patterns, plan for demand

uctuations, and optimize your inventory replenishment strategies. Minimizing stockouts improves customer satisfaction, maintains revenue streams, and enhances your brand's reliability.

On-Time Delivery:

On-time delivery measures the percentage of customer orders that are delivered within the promised or expected delivery time frame. It directly impacts customer satisfaction, loyalty, and overall business performance. Monitoring and improving on-time delivery can help mitigate stockouts, improve customer relationships, and gain a competitive advantage.

To calculate on-time delivery, divide the number of orders delivered on time by the total number of orders, and then multiply it by 100. Strive for an on-time delivery rate exceeding 95%. Analyzing on-time delivery metrics enables you to pinpoint potential bottlenecks in your supply chain, transportation, or ful llment processes. By enhancing on-time delivery, you minimize order delays, strengthen customer trust, and di erentiate yourself from your competitors.

Backorder Rate:

The backorder rate measures the percentage of customer orders that cannot be ful lled immediately due to insu cient inventory. It provides insights into the effectiveness of your inventory planning and replenishment processes. A high backorder rate may indicate the need for better inventory management strategies to prevent order delays and minimize customer dissatisfaction.

To calculate the backorder rate, divide the number of backorders by the total number of customer orders, and then multiply it by 100. Aim for a backorder rate below 5%. A high backorder rate calls for a reassessment of your demand forecasting, safety stock levels, and supply chain coordination. Reducing backorders enhances customer satisfaction, prevents lost sales, and improves overall operational efficiency.

Carrying Costs:

Carrying costs refer to the expenses associated with storing and holding inventory over a specific timeframe. It includes costs such as warehousing, insurance, handling, depreciation, obsolescence, and nancing. Monitoring and managing carrying costs are crucial to ensure adequate cash ow, optimize inventory levels, and improve pro tability.

To calculate carrying costs, determine the average inventory value and multiply it by the carrying cost rate. The carrying cost rate usually includes factors like warehouse rent, utilities, insurance, interest rates, and taxes associated with inventory holding. By measuring carrying costs, you can identify opportunities to reduce expenses through more e cient inventory control, improved demand forecasting, and strategic partnerships with suppliers.

Perfect Order Rate:

The perfect order rate measures the percentage of orders that are delivered to the customer without any errors or issues from start to nish. It encompasses various aspects such as order accuracy, on-time delivery, complete fulllment, and adherence to customer requirements. Monitoring the perfect order rate provides you with a comprehensive view of your overall order fulllment process and helps identify areas for improvement.

To calculate the perfect order rate, multiply the percentage of orders with order accuracy, on-time delivery, and complete fulllment. Aim for a perfect order rate close to 100%. Monitoring the perfect order rate allows you to streamline your order fulllment processes, minimize costs associated with order errors, improve customer satisfaction, and enhance your brand reputation.

Continuous improvement is a vital aspect of inventory management. By regularly reviewing and analyzing the performance metrics mentioned above, you can identify opportunities to improve eciency, reduce costs, and enhance customer satisfaction. Implementing process enhancements, adopting advanced inventory management technologies, and fostering a culture of continuous improvement can lead to better inventory control, increased profitability, and a competitive edge in the market.

Remember, every business is unique, so it is essential to tailor your performance metrics and continuous improvement efforts to your specific industry, business goals, and customer expectations. Regularly review and update your metrics to ensure they align with current market conditions and business objectives.

In addition to tracking and analyzing performance metrics, continuous improvement in inventory management also involves implementing best practices and adopting innovative approaches. Here are some strategies to consider:

Demand forecasting:

Improve the accuracy of your demand forecasting by leveraging historical data, market trends, customer insights, and collaboration with sales and marketing teams. Use advanced forecasting techniques and software to optimize your inventory levels, avoid stockouts, and minimize excess inventory.

Supplier management:

Establish strong relationships with your suppliers and regularly evaluate their performance. Monitor lead times, delivery reliability, quality, and pricing to ensure you have reliable and e cient supply chains. Consider implementing vendor scorecards and conducting regular supplier performance reviews.

Inventory optimization:

Analyze your inventory levels and identify opportunities to optimize them. Implement inventory segmentation techniques to prioritize high-demand and high-margin products. Consider implementing just-in-time (JIT) or lean inventory management practices to minimize carrying costs and improve order fulllment eciency.

4. Warehouse layout and organization: Optimize your warehouse layout and organization to improve eciency. Designate areas for fast-moving products, implement proper labeling and signage, and use inventory management tools like barcode scanners or RFID technology for accurate and streamlined inventory tracking. Implement ecient picking and packing processes to minimize errors and improve productivity.

5. Technology integration: Consider integrating inventory management software with other business systems such as ERP (Enterprise Resource Planning) or POS (Point of Sale) systems to ensure accurate and real-time inventory data. Use advanced analytics tools to gain insights into

inventory trends, customer behavior, and supply chain performance.

6. Cross-functional collaboration: Foster collaboration between dierent departments such as sales, marketing, operations, and nance to ensure alignment and synergy in inventory management processes. Encourage open communication, information sharing, and joint decision-making to improve forecasting accuracy, demand planning, and order fullment.

7. Continuous training and education: Invest in ongoing training and education for your inventory management team. Keep them updated on the latest industry trends, technologies, and best practices. Encourage them to attend relevant conferences, seminars, or webinars to enhance their knowledge and skills.

By implementing these strategies and continuously monitoring and improving your performance metrics, you can optimize your inventory management practices, improve customer satisfaction, reduce costs, and gain a competitive advantage in the market. Remember, inventory management is an ongoing process, and continuous improvement is key to staying ahead in a rapidly changing business environment.

Inventory Management

Chapter 3

Understanding Stress in The Modern World

Welcome to the first chapter of "Stress Less, Live More: A Blueprint for Stress Management in the Modern World." Grab a comfy seat and let's dive into the fascinating world of stress and why it seems to be everywhere in our lives.

The Stress Epidemic: A 21st Century Woe

Picture this: the modern world, a bustling hub of activity, with constant deadlines, buzzing smartphones, and a to-do list that seems to grow by the minute. Sound familiar? Well, you're not alone. Stress has become a ubiquitous companion in our daily lives, affecting people from all walks of life. But why is this the case, and what makes the stress of today different from that of yesteryears?

Stress: More Than Just a Buzzword

Let's break it down. Stress isn't just a buzzword thrown around casually; it's a physiological and psychological response ingrained in our very nature. Back in the day, stress served as a survival mechanism, helping our ancestors flee from predators or confront immediate threats. Fast forward to the 21st century, and our stressors have evolved from physical dangers to the relentless demands of our fast-paced, technology-driven lifestyles.

The Impact on Mind and Body

Now, let's talk about the impact of stress. It's not just about feeling a bit frazzled after a hectic day at work; chronic stress can take a toll on both your mind and body. From sleep disturbances and weakened immune systems to increased risk of chronic diseases, stress is like a silent saboteur working against our well-being.

Our Approach to Stress Management

But fear not! In this chapter, we're not here to add to your stress; we're here to equip you with the knowledge and tools to tackle it head-on. We'll explore the science behind stress, helping you understand why your body and mind react the way they do. Armed with this knowledge, you'll be better prepared to navigate the challenges of the modern world with grace and resilience.

Let's Get Scientific: The Physiology of Stress

So, what happens to your body when stress comes knocking? It's all about the intricate dance between your brain and body. When faced with a stressor, your brain releases a flood of hormones, including adrenaline and cortisol, gearing your body up for action. This is known as the fight-or-flight response, a primal instinct that once helped our ancestors survive, but now can leave us feeling overwhelmed and frazzled.

Understanding this physiological response is the first step to regaining control. We'll explore how chronic stress keeps this response on a constant loop, leading to a cascade of health issues. But fear not; knowledge is power, and armed with an understanding of this process, you'll be better equipped to intervene and break the cycle.

Mapping Your Stress Landscape: Identifying Stress Triggers

Now, let's get personal. What sends your stress levels through the roof? Is it that looming work deadline, the never-ending traffic, or perhaps the constant barrage of emails? In this chapter, we'll embark on a journey of self-discovery, helping you identify your unique stress triggers.

Through simple self-assessment exercises, you'll gain insights into the specific situations and circumstances that spike your stress levels. Uncovering these triggers is like shining a light in the dark; it empowers you to take targeted action, addressing the root causes of your stress rather than just managing the symptoms.

Peeling Back the Layers: Hidden Stressors

But stress isn't always straightforward. Sometimes, it hides in plain sight, disguised as everyday challenges or buried beneath the surface of our busy lives. Together, we'll explore strategies for unearthing these hidden stressors, ensuring that nothing stays in the shadows.

Armed with a clearer understanding of what's causing your stress, you'll be better equipped to create a stress management plan tailored to your unique needs. And remember, you're not alone on this journey; we're in it together, every step of the way.

Conclusion: A Journey Begins

So, here's to the start of your stress-busting adventure! In this chapter, we've laid the groundwork for understanding stress in the modern world. We've explored the roots of stress, both ancient and contemporary, and examined how it impacts your mind and body.

But this is just the beginning. In the chapters to come, we'll delve deeper into the science behind stress, explore holistic approaches to stress reduction, and guide you in crafting your personalized stress management blueprint. It's time to stress less and live more, and we're thrilled to have you on board for the ride. Stay tuned for more insights, practical tips, and a whole lot of friendly guidance as we navigate the exciting terrain of stress management together.

Chapter 4

Goals

Most successful time managers have one thing in common: they have a very clear idea of where they want to go and how they are going to get there. In this chapter we will explore how important it is to have very clear goals in both your work and personal life. We will also see how it is important to turn your goals into a plan of action and to make that plan of action flexible so it can change as circumstances change.

THE IMPORTANCE OF SETTING GOALS

When I run my training courses I usually run a session at the beginning of each course on goal setting. I will ask the delegates to write down why they are attending the training course and what they want to achieve. In response one person recently said: 'I was sent and I don't know'. In a way this was quite sad. As trainers we get people like this all the time who are negative about training and make it very obvious that they would rather be somewhere else. It is a pity that some people have such a negative attitude towards learning. Learning is a lifelong experience and one of our life goals should be to take advantage of every learning opportunity that presents itself. This example goes to show that by not setting goals we can waste opportunities to manage our time effectively.

So, why are goals important both in life and in business? As the saying goes: 'if you don't know where you are going, how are you going to know when you've got there?'

HOW LONG TERM SHOULD MY GOALS BE?

It is important to have long, medium and short-term goals. The long-term goals could be 10, or 20 years ahead depending on the particular goal. This could be something like 'I want to be financially secure by the time I am 55'. If this event is 20 years away you need to start thinking about your medium-term goals and then your short term goals. This way you have an aim in sight, but also have plans in place to get you there.

The process of goal setting is about having clear objectives, having a plan to achieve those objectives and acting on the plan, amending it as you go along. People without goals tend to achieve less than those who do have them. However, even if you have goals, you need a plan of action, and because circumstances change, your plan needs to be acted upon and amended as necessary.

CAREER GOALS

Setting goals for your career is very important. To plan your career you need to be thinking about a number of issues then putting your plan into place.

SWOT analysis

First of all, start by doing a SWOT analysis on yourself to find out the kind of career that will suit you best or to work out the parts of your job you enjoy the most. A SWOT analysis is a marketing tool that looks at:

- Strengths
- Weaknesses
- Opportunities
- Threats

Strengths: What are you good at and what do you enjoy doing? If you are the outdoor type would you suit an office job? If you are a caring person would you suit life on the trading floor of a merchant bank? Don't just take your own word for it. Ask someone you trust to give you some feedback. It is really important in your career that you enjoy what you do and are suited for your chosen profession.

Weaknesses: What are you not so good at? Are your weaknesses something you can change? Are they allowable weaknesses?

Opportunities:

What opportunities are out there that could help you build your desired career? Do you know people who could help you? Are there organisations that have resources you could tap into? A useful piece of advice to consider is that to be successful, you should find somebody who is already successful in your chosen field and mirror the things they do.

Threats:

What is stopping you from achieving your goal? Are there certain industries that don't have a long-term future? Are there outside influences that would prevent you from being successful? Might a lack of financial resources be a problem for getting into certain professions?

There are other issues to be aware of when looking at your career goals, some of which may answer some of the weaknesses or opportunities identified by your SWOT analysis.

Education and training

Some professions require education to degree level then further professional qualifications. But the education we get at school doesn't always equip us to deal with life at work. What we also find is that once we have been given a job, it is our performance, rather than formal qualifications that moves us up the career ladder. Look into any training courses you can do that will help improve your performance.

Promote yourself

It used to be that a well written CV was all that you needed. Now, with the growth of the internet, there are other ways to promote yourself. You can have your own website, and promote yourself on one or all of the social and business networking sites that we see all over the internet. Blogs are also a good way of getting you known and there are many opportunities to post articles on the internet to enhance your reputation.

Become an expert

It doesn't matter what career you choose, if you are seen as being an expert, people will find you.

Network

It is a very powerful career building tool to have a network of friends, business colleagues and contacts who can help you manage your career.

FAMILY GOALS

Many families like to sit down and plan their goals together. Individual needs change as the family grows older and when the hormones start to kick in. The goal setting process is very similar to that for your career goals, although possibly a bit more informal.

In my family we used to sit down at the beginning of each year and write a list of things we wanted to do as a family. We used to stick this list on the inside of one of the kitchen cupboard doors and cross off each item as it was achieved. Every time we opened the cupboard we got a reminder of the goal situation and it was a spur to get things done.

Make sure your family goals involve everyone and you all have a role to play in achieving them.

HEALTH GOALS

A lot of our goals can be interlinked and some can be achieved more quickly than others. Personally, most of my health goals have been based around losing weight and getting fit, although friends have looked at other health issues such as having a healthier diet and doing more exercise.

The key here is for your goals to be ambitious but achievable and realistic. For example if you set the goal of swimming a mile every day for the rest of your life, it will not happen. It is far better to set a more realistic goal that is achievable and then exceed your expectations rather than to be too ambitious and fail.

Chapter 5

The Importance of Time Management in a Busy Professional's Life

Identifying Time Wasters:

One key aspect of time management is identifying and eliminating time wasters. Several common culprits steal valuable minutes and hinder productivity. These can include excessive social media usage, unnecessary meetings, procrastination, multitasking, and disorganized workspaces, to name a few. By recognizing and addressing these time drains, you can regain control over your schedule and make better use of your limited time.

Setting Goals and Priorities:

Setting clear goals is essential for a busy professional seeking success. Time management becomes more effective when you have a well-defined purpose and direction. By establishing both short-term and long-term goals, you can align your tasks and activities accordingly, ensuring you make progress towards your desired outcomes. Prioritizing these goals helps you allocate time and energy to the most important tasks, avoiding the trap of being busy but not productive.

Tools and Strategies for Time Management:

In this chapter, we will explore various tools and strategies that can aid in effective time management. From utilizing digital calendars and task management apps to employing techniques such as the Pomodoro Technique and Eisenhower Matrix, there are numerous approaches to enhance your time management skills. Understanding these tools and techniques will empower you to optimize your daily routine, streamline your tasks, and achieve optimal productivity as a busy professional.

CHAPTER 6

Basics of Time

Overview

How do you maximize the time that you have?

Have you ever felt as though you could have accomplished more with your time but were unable to do so at the end of the day? For most people, this scene is probably typical. However, you must understand that time management is a necessary component of success.

The Foundations of Time Management

One of the most important things in life is said to be time.

The modern society would be in serious trouble without it. For this reason, a lot of people make an effort to manage their time well.

Effective time management is widely regarded as the most critical component of becoming a successful worker, learner, or individual.

Before you read any further, consider this: what do you do on a daily basis to effectively manage your own time? Have you ever found yourself stumbling through other activities during the course of a day while working on a particular task? Have you ever combined two distinct tasks—successfully or unsuccessfully?

When you're lying in bed, do you find yourself thinking about what you ought to have done today? In such a case, it can be a positive indication since you are cognizant of your own time, at least.

So what exactly is time management? To put it simply, time management is the skill of planning your days' worth of duties and managing your schedule such that you may logically and successfully do all of them in addition to your personal activities.

You have to approach time management on a variety of levels.

If you can manage an unexpected task that is not on your daily routine, then you can consider yourself an efficient time manager. You need to get knowledgeable about proper time management because this is the precise point at when it becomes relevant.

For the time being, though, all it takes to create an effective calendar is setting aside one day a week—ideally a weekend day—to spend one or more hours sitting down with yourself and creating a weekly agenda. As you work on this, make a list of the things you need to get done each day and figure out how long it will take you to finish them.

Don't deceive yourself by adding impossibilities.

Verify that the schedule you have made corresponds to actual events. As you create the schedule, you could envision how it would operate in your head.

Yes, initially, anticipate that it will be challenging. But remember that mastering time management will undoubtedly assist you greatly in all spheres of your life, including job and education.

And in the unlikely event that you struggle to commit to it, never forget that time is your most valuable asset, which you should always manage well. Even though time is valuable, people must earn it; unlike money, which you can have whatever you like. Make the most of it because once you lose it, you can never get it back.

Time management is the process of organizing and planning how to allocate your time between different tasks and activities. It allows you to work smarter, not harder, leading to greater productivity and reduced stress.

Time management is a dance. It's about finding the rhythm that works for you and moving gracefully through your day. It's about knowing when to say yes and when to say no, and about making the most of the time that you have.

Time management is the superpower that helps you achieve more in less time. It's the ability to plan, organize, and prioritize your tasks so that you can focus on the most important things and get them done efficiently.

Good time management is essential for success in all areas of life. It can help you to reduce stress, increase productivity, and achieve your goals more quickly. On the other hand, poor time management can lead to missed deadlines, increased stress, and a feeling of overwhelm.

Time management is a improved with practice. management techniques and tools available, so you can find a system that works for you.

skill that can be learned and

There are many different time

Time management is the art of using your time wisely to achieve your goals. It's about planning, organizing, and prioritizing your tasks so that you can work smarter, not harder.

CHAPTER 7

The benefits of good time management include:

Increased productivity

Reduced stress

More free time to do the things you love

Effective time management is essential for project success. We all have the same 24 hours in a day, but some people seem to achieve more than others. This is often because they have better time management skills.

If you feel overwhelmed by your workload or anxious about incomplete tasks, it's time to focus on developing effective time management strategies. Here are a few tips:

Plan your day ahead of time. Decide what tasks you need to complete and prioritize them. Set realistic deadlines for yourself.

Break down large tasks into smaller, more manageable ones. This will make them seem less daunting and help you stay on track.

Schedule time for each task and stick to your schedule as much as possible. Avoid distractions and take breaks when you need them.

Delegate tasks to others whenever possible. This will free up your time so you can focus on the most important tasks.

Say no to new commitments if you don't have the time to take them on. It's better to focus on completing the tasks you already have than to start new ones and risk spreading yourself too thin.

Remember, time management is a skill that takes time and practice to develop. Don't get discouraged if you don't see results immediately. Just keep working at it and you'll eventually find a system that works for you.

*T*ime management is a skill that can be learned and improved, and it can have a positive impact on every area of your life. Whether you're a student, a stay-at-home parent, or a corporate executive, effective time management can help you to:

Here are some tips for managing your time more efficiently:

Set goals and priorities: What do you want to achieve in the short-term and long-term? Once you know your goals, you can start to prioritize your tasks and focus on the most important ones.

Plan your time : Once you have your priorities, create a schedule for yourself. This will help you to stay on track and avoid distractions.

Break down large tasks into smaller ones: This will make them seem less daunting and more manageable.

Take breaks:

It's important to take breaks throughout the day, even if it's just for a few minutes. This will help you to stay focused and productive when you're working.

- Delegate tasks:

If you have the ability to delegate tasks, do it! This will free up your time so that you can focus on the most important things.

- **Reward yourself.** When you complete a task or reach a goal, reward yourself! This will help you to stay motivated and on track.

By following these tips, you can improve your time management skills and get more done in less time.

Time management is a skill that takes practice to develop. But by following these tips, you can start to improve your time management skills and get more done in less time.

Key Principles of Time Management

A. Prioritization

Importance of identifying and focusing on high-priority tasks

Identifying and focusing on high-priority tasks is essential for maximizing productivity, achieving goals, and maintaining a sense of control over one's time and responsibilities. The importance of this practice cannot be overstated, and here are some key reasons why it is crucial:

Efficient Resource Allocation: Time and energy are finite resources. Identifying high-priority tasks ensures that these valuable resources are channeled towards activities that align with strategic objectives and yield the greatest returns.

Goal Achievement: High-priority tasks are often directly related to the accomplishment of important goals. By focusing on these tasks, individuals can make significant progress and stay on track to achieve their targets.

Time Optimization: Prioritizing tasks allows individuals to optimize their time. Rather than getting lost in low-impact or non-essential activities, they can concentrate on tasks that have a direct impact on their success.

Reducing Overwhelm: When faced with a long list of tasks, it's easy to feel overwhelmed. Identifying high-priority tasks breaks the workload into manageable chunks, making it less daunting and more achievable.

Meeting Deadlines: **High-priority tasks often come with deadlines or time constraints. By giving these tasks the attention they deserve, individuals can meet deadlines and avoid last-minute rushes.**

Improved Decision-Making: Prioritization involves evaluating tasks based on their importance and urgency. This process enhances decision-making skills, ensuring that individuals invest their time in the most valuable activities.

Enhancing Focus and Concentration: Focusing on high-priority tasks allows individuals to channel their focus and concentration. This dedicated attention leads to better-quality work and more efficient task completion.

Stress Reduction: Knowing what needs to be done and tackling high-priority tasks in a structured manner reduces stress and anxiety. It provides a sense of direction and control over one's workload.

Seizing Opportunities: Prioritization leaves room for seizing unexpected opportunities that align with overarching goals. When core responsibilities are managed efficiently, individuals can explore new prospects and avenues for growth.

Building Momentum: Accomplishing high-priority tasks creates momentum and motivation to tackle other tasks on the list. It fosters a sense of achievement and propels individuals towards greater productivity.

1 **Enhancing Professional Reputation:** Consistently focusing on high-priority tasks leads to a reputation for reliability and competence. This can open doors for new opportunities and career advancements.

1 W**ork-Life Balance:** Prioritizing tasks allows individuals to create a better work-life balance. By efficiently completing crucial work, they can make time for personal life, hobbies, and self-care.

In conclusion, identifying and focusing on high-priority tasks is critical for success in personal and professional life. It enables individuals to optimize their time, achieve their goals, and maintain a healthy balance between their various responsibilities. By mastering the skill of prioritization, individuals can become more productive, efficient, and successful in their endeavors.

CHAPTER 8

Techniques for evaluating task importance and urgency

Evaluating task importance and urgency is a vital step in effective time management. Several techniques can help individuals assess the significance and time-sensitivity of tasks to prioritize them accordingly:

Eisenhower Matrix: This technique categorizes tasks based on their importance and urgency into four quadrants:

Important and Urgent:

Tasks that require immediate attention and have significant consequences if not addressed promptly.

Important but Not Urgent:

Tasks that are crucial but don't require immediate action. These should be scheduled and planned for completion.

Urgent but Not Important:

Tasks that demand immediate attention but have minimal impact on long-term goals. Delegation or elimination is often considered for these tasks.

Not Important and Not Urgent:

Tasks that are low priority and don't contribute significantly to goals. Minimize or eliminate these tasks whenever possible.

Tasks:

High priority and high urgency tasks that need immediate attention.

Tasks:

High priority but lower urgency tasks that should be planned for completion.

Tasks: Lower priority but high urgency tasks that may require delegation or quick execution.

Tasks: Low priority and low urgency tasks that can be deprioritized or eliminated.

VALUE-DEADLINE MATRIX:

This method involves plotting tasks on a matrix based on their value and deadline:

High-Value, Near Deadline:

Tasks that are valuable and have imminent deadlines require immediate action.

High-Value, Distant Deadline:

Important tasks with more extended timelines can be planned and scheduled.

Low-Value, Near Deadline:

Tasks with little impact and tight deadlines may be delegated or streamlined.

Low-Value, Distant Deadline:

Low-priority tasks with more extended timelines can be postponed or eliminated.

Goal Setting

Setting SMART goals to provide clarity and direction

Setting Smart Goals Is A Powerful Technique That Provides Clarity And Direction To Individuals, Teams, And Organizations. SMART Is An Acronym That Stands For Specific, Measurable, Achievable, Relevant, And Time-Bound. When Goals Are Defined Using These Criteria, They Become More Focused And Actionable, Increasing The Likelihood Of Success. Let's Explore Each Aspect Of SMART Goals:

Specific: A Specific Goal Is Clear And Well-Defined. It Answers The What And "How" Of The Objective. Specific Goals Leave No Room For

Ambiguity, Ensuring Everyone Involved Understands The Intended Outcome.

Measurable:

A measurable goal includes criteria that allow progress and success to be objectively assessed. Measuring progress provides motivation and helps individuals stay on track. For example, "Increase customer satisfaction ratings from 80% to 90% within six months.

Achievable:

An achievable goal is realistic and within reach. It considers available resources, skills, and time frames to ensure that the goal can be accomplished. Setting unrealistic goals can lead to frustration and demotivation. For example, "Expand to 50 new international markets within a month" may not be achievable given practical constraints.

Relevant:

A relevant goal aligns with the broader objectives and priorities of individuals or organizations. It ensures that the efforts put into achieving the goal contribute to overall success and are meaningful. For example, a goal related to product development would be relevant for a company in the tech industry but not for a restaurant.

Time-bound:

A time-bound goal has a specific deadline for completion. This provides a sense of urgency and helps individuals stay focused on meeting the timeline. It also enables progress tracking and ensures accountability. For example, "Launch the new product line by the end of the fiscal year."

By setting **SMART** goals, individuals and organizations gain several benefits:

Clarity:

Smart goals provide clear and precise objectives, reducing confusion and increasing understanding among team members.

Focus:

The specificity and measurability of SMART goals help individuals stay focused on what needs to be done to achieve the desired outcome.

Motivation:

Achievable goals with clear deadlines create a sense of motivation and enthusiasm among individuals, driving them towards success.

Accountability:

The time-bound aspect of SMART goals fosters accountability, as progress can be measured against set deadlines.

Success-oriented mindset:

Smart goals provide a roadmap for success, allowing individuals to track their progress and celebrate achievements along the way.

In conclusion, setting SMART goals is a valuable practice to provide clarity and direction for individuals and organizations. By being specific, measurable, achievable, relevant, and time-bound, SMART goals empower individuals to stay on course, maintain focus, and achieve meaningful and attainable objectives.

CHAPTER 9

Breaking down long-term goals into manageable tasks

Breaking down long-term goals into manageable tasks is a crucial step in making those goals achievable and less overwhelming. Long-term goals can be ambitious and complex, and without proper planning, they may seem unattainable. By breaking them down into smaller, actionable tasks, individuals can create a roadmap for success and maintain momentum towards their desired outcomes. Here's how to effectively break down long-term goals:

Start with the End Goal:

Clearly define the long-term goal and have a clear picture of what success looks like. This serves as the anchor for the entire process.

Identify Milestones:

Break the long-term goal into significant milestones or checkpoints. These are intermediate goals that mark progress and give a sense of accomplishment along the way.

Create Short-Term Objectives:

Based on the milestones, set short-term objectives that lead to achieving each milestone. These objectives should be more specific and actionable.

Set Specific Tasks:

For each short-term objective, define specific tasks that need to be completed. Be clear about what needs to be done and what resources are required.

Prioritize Tasks:

Determine the order in which tasks should be completed, taking into consideration dependencies and deadlines.

Assign Timeframes:

Attach timeframes or deadlines to each task to create a sense of urgency and maintain focus.

Be Realistic:

Ensure that the breakdown of tasks is achievable and realistic given available resources and constraints.

Monitor and Adjust:

Regularly review progress and make adjustments to the plan if necessary. Flexibility is essential when dealing with long-term goals.

Use Project Management Tools:

Consider using project management tools or task management apps to track progress and keep everyone involved on the same page.

Celebrate Milestones: Celebrate the completion of milestones and acknowledge the progress made towards the long-term goal. Celebrations provide motivation and reinforce the commitment to reaching the end goal.

Breaking down long-term goals into manageable tasks not only makes them less daunting but also helps to maintain focus and momentum. It allows individuals to stay organized and track progress effectively, making it easier to stay on course and achieve success. With a well-structured plan in place, individuals are better equipped to overcome challenges and stay committed to the journey towards achieving their long-term objectives.

Time Blocking

Allocating specific time slots for different activities

Allocating specific time slots for different activities is a foundational time management technique that can significantly boost productivity and help individuals make the most of their day. By creating a well-structured schedule, individuals can ensure that each activity receives the attention it deserves and minimize the risk of wasting time. Here are some steps to effectively allocate time slots for different activities:

Identify Priorities: Determine the most important tasks and activities that need to be accomplished during the day. Prioritization ensures that essential activities are given sufficient time and attention.

Create a To-Do List: List down all the tasks and activities that need to be completed, both personal and professional. Having a comprehensive to-do list helps individuals visualize their day.

Estimate Time Needed: Estimate the amount of time required for each task. Be realistic and consider any potential interruptions or unforeseen circumstances.

Categorize Activities:

Group similar activities together. For example, allocate specific time slots for focused work, meetings, emails, personal errands, breaks, etc.

Use Time Blocking:

Time blocking involves setting aside specific time blocks for each category of activities. For example, allocate a 2-hour block for focused work on a project, followed by a 30-minute break, and then a 1-hour block for emails.

Be Flexible but Stick to the Schedule:

While it's essential to be flexible in case of unexpected events, try to adhere to the allocated time slots as much as possible. This helps maintain a sense of structure and discipline.

Consider Peak Productivity Times:

Identify your peak productivity hours, and schedule the most challenging and important tasks during this period when you're at your best.

Avoid Multitasking:

Focus on one activity at a time during each time block. Multitasking can reduce efficiency and lead to increased mental fatigue.

Prioritize Self-Care:

Allocate time for self-care activities like exercise, meditation, or hobbies. Taking care of yourself is essential for maintaining overall well-being and productivity.

Review and Adjust:

Regularly review your schedule and assess whether the allocated time slots are realistic and effective. Make adjustments as needed to optimize your time usage.

Avoid Overloading:

Be mindful not to over-schedule yourself. Leave some buffer time between activities to handle unexpected tasks or simply to take a breather.

Use Time Management Tools:

Consider using digital calendars, task management apps, or planners to help organize and visualize your schedule effectively.

By allocating specific time slots for different activities, individuals can enhance their time management skills, reduce procrastination, and maintain a sense of control over their daily routines. A well-planned schedule ensures that each task is given adequate attention, leading to increased productivity and a greater sense of accomplishment.

Benefits of creating a structured schedule

Creating a structured schedule offers numerous benefits that can significantly improve productivity, reduce stress, and enhance overall well-being. Here are some key advantages of having a well-organized and structured schedule:

Increased Productivity:

A structured schedule ensures that time is allocated efficiently, allowing individuals to focus on essential tasks and avoid time-wasting activities. This increased productivity leads to more significant accomplishments and goal achievement.

Time Optimization:

A structured schedule helps individuals make the most of their available time. By allocating specific time slots for different activities, they can ensure that each task receives the attention it deserves and that no time is wasted on indecision or disorganization.

Improved Time Management:

Following a structured schedule fosters better time management skills. It encourages individuals to prioritize tasks, set clear objectives, and allocate time based on their importance and urgency.

Reduced Stress and Anxiety:

Knowing what needs to be done and having a plan to tackle tasks reduces stress and anxiety. A structured schedule provides a sense of control and certainty, alleviating the feeling of being overwhelmed by a long list of to-dos.

Enhanced Focus and Concentration:

A structured schedule promotes better focus and concentration. When individuals know what to work on during specific time blocks, they are less likely to get distracted and more likely to maintain attention on the task at hand.

Greater Accountability:

A structured schedule holds individuals accountable for their time. When tasks are clearly defined and time-bound, individuals are more likely to adhere to their commitments and meet deadlines.

Better Work-Life Balance:

Structured scheduling helps individuals create a balance between work and personal life. By allocating specific time for work, family, hobbies, and self-care, they can maintain a healthier and more fulfilling lifestyle.

Increased Efficiency:

A well-organized schedule helps individuals identify potential inefficiencies and time-wasting habits. With this awareness, they can make necessary adjustments and become more efficient in their daily routines.

Improved Decision-Making:

A structured schedule involves making choices about how to allocate time to various activities. This process enhances decision-making skills, ensuring that individuals focus on what truly matters and avoid being sidetracked by less important tasks.

Sense of Accomplishment:

Following a structured schedule provides a sense of accomplishment as tasks are completed within allocated time frames. This feeling of progress and achievement contributes to greater motivation and satisfaction.

Flexibility and Adaptability:

While a structured schedule provides a clear plan, it also allows for flexibility and adaptability. Individuals can adjust their schedules to accommodate unexpected events or changes in priorities.

Time for Personal Growth:

By including time for self-improvement and personal development in the schedule, individuals can allocate time to learn new skills, pursue hobbies, or engage in activities that contribute to their growth and well-being.

In conclusion, creating a structured schedule offers a myriad of benefits that positively impact productivity, time management, stress levels, and work-life balance. It empowers individuals to make better use of their time, stay organized, and achieve their goals with greater efficiency and effectiveness.

CHAPTER 10

Understanding Time Management:

.

Key Components:

Prioritization: Recognize the importance of different tasks and allocate time based on their significance. Not all tasks are equal, and prioritizing ensures that you focus on what truly matters.

Goal Setting: Time management is closely linked to setting clear, specific, and achievable goals. Knowing what you want to accomplish allows you to allocate time according to your priorities.

Self-Awareness: Understand your own habits, strengths, and weaknesses. A clear understanding of your working style helps in creating a time management plan that suits your needs.

Planning: Effective planning involves breaking down larger goals into smaller, manageable tasks. It helps create a roadmap for your activities and reduces the likelihood of feeling overwhelmed.

Flexibility: Despite meticulous planning, unexpected events can occur. Being adaptable and able to adjust your schedule allows for a more realistic and sustainable approach to time management.

Eliminating Time Wasters: Identify and minimize activities that consume time without contributing significantly to your goals. This may involve managing distractions, setting boundaries, and learning to say no when necessary.

Regular Evaluation: Reflect on your time management practices regularly. Assess what is working well and what could be improved. Continuous evaluation allows for refinement and adjustment as needed.

In essence, understanding time management is about making intentional choices about how you spend your time. It empowers you to be proactive, organized, and in control of your daily activities, leading to increased efficiency and a greater sense of accomplishment.

Balanced Lifestyle: Time management ensures a balance between work, family, hobbies, and personal growth. It contributes to a fulfilling and harmonious life, preventing burnout and stress.

Goal Achievement: Individuals can pursue personal goals and aspirations by allocating time deliberately. Whether it's learning a new skill, exercising, or spending quality time with loved ones, effective time management propels personal growth.

3.Stress Reduction: Prioritizing tasks and managing time efficiently reduces the stress associated with missed deadlines and chaotic schedules. It fosters a sense of control and accomplishment.

Quality Relationships: Spending quality time with family and friends is essential for nurturing relationships. Time management ensures that meaningful connections are prioritized amid life's demands.

Productivity: Time management is synonymous with heightened productivity. Prioritizing tasks and avoiding procrastination lead to efficient work processes and increased output.

Meeting Deadlines: Meeting deadlines is critical in the professional realm. Effective time management ensures that projects are completed on time, enhancing reliability and reputation.

Career Advancement: Individuals who manage their time effectively often stand out in the workplace. They demonstrate organizational skills, reliability, and the ability to handle multiple responsibilities, contributing to career advancement.

Work-Life Balance: A well-managed schedule in the professional domain allows for a healthier work-life balance. This balance is vital for sustained performance, job satisfaction, and overall well-being.

In essence, effective time management is a cornerstone for holistic success. It empowers individuals to navigate the complexities of personal and professional life, fostering achievement, fulfillment, and a sense of control in the face of life's demands.

Excessive Social Media Use: Endless scrolling and frequent social media checks can consume significant chunks of time, diverting attention from essential tasks.

Procrastination: Delaying tasks that need attention contributes to time wastage.

Recognizing and overcoming procrastination is key to efficient time management.

3.Unnecessary Meetings: Meetings without clear agendas or those that could be handled through other means often lead to time inefficiencies. Identifying when a meeting is truly essential helps streamline communication.

Multitasking: Contrary to popular belief, multitasking can be counterproductive. Juggling multiple tasks simultaneously may reduce focus and overall efficiency.

5.Email Overload: Constantly checking and responding to emails throughout the day can be a significant time drain. Prioritizing emails and establishing designated times for communication can mitigate this.

Chapter 11

Understanding Time Management Fundamentals

Time, an intangible yet invaluable resource, serves as the currency of productivity, success, and personal fulfillment. Its elusive nature often leaves us scrambling to grasp its essence, prompting the need for effective time management. This foundational concept forms the bedrock of efficiency, enabling individuals to navigate life's complexities while maximizing their potential.

At its core, time management transcends mere scheduling; it embodies a holistic approach encompassing prioritization, organization, and self-discipline. It entails not just allocating time but allocating it purposefully, aligning actions with objectives to yield optimal outcomes. In essence, it's the art of balancing responsibilities, desires, and obligations against the ticking hands of the clock.

The significance of mastering time management reverberates across all facets of life. Professionally, it delineates the boundary between productivity and chaos. A well-structured approach empowers individuals to meet deadlines, enhance quality, and foster innovation. It breeds a culture of efficiency within organizations, catalyzing growth and success.

On a personal level, effective time management nurtures a harmonious life balance. It allows for the pursuit of passions, the nurturing of relationships, and the cultivation of personal growth. By allocating time intentionally, individuals unlock the potential for self-improvement, pursuing hobbies, and fostering mental and physical well-being.

However, the journey towards mastering time management is not without challenges. Procrastination, distractions, and overcommitment often sabotage well-intended plans. Hence, the need for strategies such as prioritization, goal setting, and the establishment of boundaries becomes imperative. Learning to say 'no' when necessary and employing techniques like the Pomodoro Technique or Eisenhower Matrix can be invaluable tools in this pursuit.

Moreover, technological advancements have both aided and complicated time management. While digital tools offer unprecedented assistance in organizing schedules and tasks, they also pose the risk of becoming distractions themselves. Hence, fostering a mindful approach to technology usage is crucial in optimizing its benefits without succumbing to its pitfalls.

In essence, effective time management serves as a compass, guiding individuals through the maze of modern-day demands. It's about taking charge of one's time, making deliberate choices, and ensuring that each moment contributes meaningfully to the overarching tapestry of life. The journey towards mastering this art is ongoing, requiring continuous introspection, adaptability, and a commitment to self-improvement.

Ultimately, understanding the fundamentals of time management transcends the confines of a mere skill; it embodies a philosophy that empowers individuals to seize control of their destinies and sculpt a life that resonates with purpose and fulfillment.

Effective time management is often hindered by various misconceptions and barriers that impede individuals from optimizing their use of time.

Identifying these obstacles is crucial in developing strategies to overcome them. Here are some common misconceptions and barriers:

Misconceptions:

1. Time is Limitless: One prevalent misconception is viewing time as an infinite resource. Believing there's always tomorrow can lead to procrastination and neglect of immediate tasks.

2. Busyness Equals Productivity: Many equate a packed schedule with productivity. However, busyness doesn't always translate to meaningful progress. It's about quality over quantity.

3. One-size-fits-all Approach: Assuming that a single time management technique works universally for everyone disregards individual differences in work styles, preferences, and priorities.

4. Overemphasis on Planning: While planning is crucial, an excessive focus on perfecting plans can

become a barrier to action, leading to procrastination.

5. Technology Solves Everything: Relying solely on technology for time management can create distractions, as excessive use of apps or devices might hinder productivity rather than enhance it.

Barriers:

1. Procrastination: Delaying tasks due to lack of motivation, fear of failure, or a desire for perfectionism undermines effective time management.

2. Lack of Prioritization: Not distinguishing between urgent and important tasks can lead to spending time on trivial matters while neglecting crucial ones.

3. Poor Delegation and Saying "No": Reluctance to delegate tasks or say 'no' to additional

responsibilities can lead to overcommitment and time fragmentation.

4. Interruptions and Distractions: Constant interruptions, be it from emails, social media, or colleagues, disrupt focus and productivity.

5. Unrealistic Time Estimation: Underestimating the time required to complete tasks leads to poor planning and an overwhelming workload.

Recognizing and addressing these misconceptions and barriers is pivotal in developing effective time management habits. Strategies such as setting realistic goals, prioritizing tasks, creating structured schedules, embracing delegation, minimizing distractions, and adopting time estimation techniques can greatly enhance one's ability to manage time efficiently. Additionally, fostering a mindset shift towards viewing time as a finite and precious resource encourages a more intentional and mindful approach to its utilization.

Boosting productivity involves adopting key principles and approaches that enhance efficiency and effectiveness in how time and effort are utilized. Here are some fundamental principles and approaches for better productivity:

Key Principles:

1. Prioritization: Identifying and focusing on high-value tasks is crucial. The Eisenhower Matrix, categorizing tasks into urgent, important, not urgent, and not important, helps prioritize effectively.

2. Time Blocking: Dedicate specific blocks of time to certain tasks or categories of work. This minimizes distractions and promotes deep focus on the task at hand.

3. Goal Setting: Establish clear, achievable, and measurable goals. Break them down into smaller, manageable steps to track progress and maintain motivation.

4. The 80/20 Rule (Pareto Principle): Acknowledge that roughly 80% of results come from 20% of efforts. Identify and focus on the most impactful tasks that yield the greatest outcomes.

5. Continuous Improvement: Embrace a growth mindset, seeking ways to refine processes, learn new skills, and optimize workflows consistently.

Approaches:

1. Time Management Techniques: Implement strategies like the Pomodoro Technique (working in focused intervals with short breaks), batching similar tasks together, or the "Two-Minute Rule" (if a task takes less than two minutes, do it immediately).

2. Single-tasking: Contrary to multitasking, which can reduce efficiency, focus on one task at a time to achieve better quality results and heightened concentration.

3. Effective Communication: Streamline communication channels, set clear expectations, and minimize unnecessary meetings to save time and enhance collaboration.

4. Automation and Delegation: Identify tasks that can be automated using tools or software, and delegate tasks when feasible to free up time for higher-value work.

5. Mindfulness and Breaks: Encourage mindfulness practices like meditation or regular breaks to recharge and maintain mental clarity, ultimately enhancing productivity.

Adopting these principles and approaches isn't a one-size-fits-all solution. It's essential to experiment and tailor these strategies to individual preferences and work styles. Consistency, adaptability, and a willingness to refine these practices over time play a crucial role in achieving sustained productivity gains.

CHAPTER 12

RECOGNIZING TIME MANAGEMENT

Time, our lives' elusive and ethereal currency, is a resource that we all share in equal measure. The way we manage this resource might mean the difference between a chaotic, overwhelming existence and a life filled with successes, fulfillment, and balance. This chapter delves into the principles of time management, investigating its relevance, the psychology underlying our perception of time, and the major obstacles that frequently impede our control of this valuable asset.

What exactly is time management?

Time management is, at its foundation, the deliberate and purposeful process of planning, organizing, and allocating your time to tasks and activities. It is the art of making purposeful choices about how you spend each minute in order to maximize productivity and achieve your goals. Time management is about doing the right things at the appropriate time, not just doing more.

The Importance of Good Time Management

Why is time management important? Consider a day with no organization or plan—tasks that are left unfinished, deadlines that are missed, and a perpetual sense of desperation. The cure to chaos is effective time management. It gives you

The ability to manage your time, prioritize projects, and devote time to activities that correspond with your objectives and beliefs.

Consider how time management affects not just productivity but also your whole well-being as we investigate its relevance. When time is well handled, stress levels fall, decision-making improves, and a sense of achievement prevails. It is more than simply a tool for professionals attempting to meet deadlines; it is the foundation of a healthy and fulfilled existence.

INVESTIGATING TIME PERCEPTION PSYCOLOGY

Time as a Personal Experience

Have you ever noticed how time appears to fly by while you're engaged in a pleasurable pastime, but drags when you're bored or anxious? Our emotions, focus, and the nature of the activity at hand all impact our experience of time. Understanding this psychological aspect of time is essential for good time management.

www.ingramcontent.com/pod-product-compliance
Lightning Source LLC
LaVergne TN
LVHW010552070526
838199LV00063BA/4955